M000032977

YOU

do

YOU

summersdale

YOU DO YOU

An Hachette UK Company
www.hachette.co.uk

Summersdale Publishers Ltd
Part of Octopus Publishing Group Limited
Carmelite House
50 Victoria Embankment
LONDON
EC4Y 0DZ
UK

www.summersdale.com

Printed and bound in China

ISBN: 978-1-78783-259-6

Substantial discounts on bulk quantities of Summersdale books are available to corporations, professional associations and other organizations. For details contact general enquiries: telephone: +44 (0) 1243 771107 or email: enquiries@summersdale.com.

TO.............................

FROM...........................

TO BE YOURSELF
IN A WORLD THAT IS
CONSTANTLY TRYING
TO MAKE YOU
SOMETHING ELSE
IS THE GREATEST
ACCOMPLISHMENT.

RALPH WALDO EMERSON

LIVE LIFE TO THE FULLEST AND FOCUS ON THE POSITIVE.

MATT CAMERON

I WILL

embrace

EVERY DAY

of my

LIFE

JUST ENJOY EVERY MOMENT – DON'T STRESS. JUST BE YOURSELF.

MABEL

YOU ARE
MAGNIFICENT
BEYOND MEASURE,
PERFECT IN YOUR
IMPERFECTIONS,
AND WONDERFULLY
MADE.

ABIOLA ABRAMS

Treat yourself right

IT'S NEVER
TOO LATE TO
TAKE A LEAP
OF FAITH AND
SEE WHAT WILL
HAPPEN – AND
TO BE BRAVE
IN LIFE.

JANE FONDA

BETTER TO
LIVE ONE YEAR
AS A TIGER,
THAN A HUNDRED
AS A SHEEP.

MADONNA

Sometimes courage
is the quiet voice
at the end of
the day saying,
"I will try again
tomorrow."

MARY ANNE RADMACHER

ONCE YOU FIGURE OUT WHO YOU ARE AND WHAT YOU LOVE ABOUT YOURSELF, IT ALL KIND OF FALLS INTO PLACE.

JENNIFER ANISTON

BELIEVE

in

YOURSELF

THE WAY YOU CARRY YOURSELF IS INFLUENCED BY THE WAY YOU FEEL INSIDE.

MARILYN MONROE

BE YOURSELF...
IT REALLY
DOESN'T MATTER
WHAT OTHER
PEOPLE THINK.

TAYLOR SCHILLING

I AM

STRONG,

CONFIDENT

AND

POWERFUL

TO SUCCEED
IN LIFE, YOU
NEED THREE
THINGS:
A WISHBONE,
A BACKBONE
AND A
FUNNY BONE.

REBA McENTIRE

WE BECOME WHAT WE THINK ABOUT.

EARL NIGHTINGALE

DON'T FOCUS ON
NEGATIVE THINGS;
FOCUS ON THE
POSITIVE, AND YOU
WILL FLOURISH.

ALEK WEK

*My mission in
life is not merely
to survive, but to
thrive; and to do so
with some passion,
some compassion,
some humour
and some style.*

MAYA ANGELOU

Do what makes you happy

WHEN YOU HAVE CONFIDENCE, YOU CAN HAVE A LOT OF FUN.

JOE NAMATH

TO ACCOMPLISH
GREAT THINGS,
WE MUST NOT
ONLY ACT,
BUT ALSO DREAM;
NOT ONLY PLAN,
BUT ALSO
BELIEVE.

ANATOLE FRANCE

All

you

need

is

you

LIFE IS 10 PER CENT WHAT HAPPENS TO YOU AND 90 PER CENT HOW YOU REACT TO IT.

CHARLES R. SWINDOLL

THE SECRET TO SUCCESS IS TO BE YOURSELF.

S. SREESANTH

ADVENTURE IS WORTHWHILE IN ITSELF.

AMELIA EARHART

MANY OF LIFE'S
FAILURES ARE
PEOPLE WHO DID
NOT REALIZE HOW
CLOSE THEY WERE
TO SUCCESS
WHEN THEY
GAVE UP.

THOMAS EDISON

THE SCARIEST MOMENT IS ALWAYS JUST BEFORE YOU START.

STEPHEN KING

DO A

LITTLE THING

CALLED

"WHAT YOU

WANT"

*Find out
who you are and
be that person –
Find that truth,
live that truth and
everything else
will come.*

ELLEN DeGENERES

**YOUR TIME
IS LIMITED,
SO DON'T
WASTE IT
LIVING
SOMEONE
ELSE'S LIFE.**

STEVE JOBS

HONESTLY,
IT'S REALLY FUN
TO BE YOURSELF.

ADAM RIPPON

Love

yourself

first

BE FAITHFUL TO THAT WHICH EXISTS NOWHERE BUT IN YOURSELF.

ANDRÉ GIDE

THE QUESTION ISN'T WHO'S GOING TO LET ME; IT'S WHO'S GOING TO STOP ME.

AYN RAND

ACT AS IF
WHAT YOU DO
MAKES A
DIFFERENCE.
IT DOES.

WILLIAM JAMES

LOVE YOUR
FLAWS. OWN YOUR
QUIRKS. AND KNOW
THAT YOU ARE
JUST AS PERFECT
AS ANYONE
ELSE, EXACTLY
AS YOU ARE.

ARIANA GRANDE

I AM COMPLETELY MYSELF – WHAT'S YOUR SUPERPOWER?

There are multiple sides to all of us. Who we are – and who we might be if we follow our dreams.

MILEY CYRUS

WE ARE EACH MADE DIFFERENTLY, SO FIND WHATEVER FLAW OR IMPERFECTION YOU HAVE AND START EMBRACING IT BECAUSE IT'S PART OF YOU.

DEMI LOVATO

GREAT THINGS

NEVER COME

FROM THE

COMFORT

ZONE

JUST BE YOURSELF, THERE IS NO ONE BETTER.

TAYLOR SWIFT

HIDE NOT YOUR TALENTS. THEY FOR USE WERE MADE. WHAT'S A SUNDIAL IN THE SHADE?

BENJAMIN FRANKLIN

THE MORE WE DO, THE MORE WE CAN DO.

WILLIAM HAZLITT

SOME PEOPLE
SAY YOU ARE
GOING THE
WRONG WAY,
WHEN IT'S
SIMPLY A WAY
OF YOUR OWN.

ANGELINA JOLIE

LET *your* INNER *light* SHINE!

YOU CAN'T BE
HESITANT ABOUT
WHO YOU ARE.

VIOLA DAVIS

BE

the best

VERSION

of

YOU

My beauty is not about how I look. My beauty is about my heart and soul.

LAVERNE COX

IF YOU ASK
ME WHAT I
CAME INTO
THIS LIFE TO
DO, I WILL
TELL YOU:
I CAME TO
LIVE OUT
LOUD.

ÉMILE ZOLA

EVERY MAN IS THE ARCHITECT OF HIS OWN FORTUNE.

APPIUS CLAUDIUS CAECUS

I'M NOT BOSSY,
I'M THE BOSS.

BEYONCÉ

Life is made for living, so get out there!

ACT THE WAY YOU WANT TO FEEL.

GRETCHEN RUBIN

ALWAYS GO
WITH YOUR
PASSIONS.
NEVER ASK
YOURSELF IF
IT'S REALISTIC
OR NOT.

DEEPAK CHOPRA

Stop holding back just because the others can't keep up

NO ONE CAN
MAKE YOU FEEL
INFERIOR WITHOUT
YOUR CONSENT.

ELEANOR ROOSEVELT

Set your goals high, and don't stop until you get there.

BO JACKSON

IT TAKES COURAGE TO GROW UP AND BECOME WHO YOU REALLY ARE.

E. E. CUMMINGS

IT IS CONFIDENCE IN OUR BODIES, MINDS AND SPIRITS THAT ALLOWS US TO KEEP LOOKING FOR NEW ADVENTURES.

OPRAH WINFREY

BE SURE

TO TAKE

ENOUGH

VITAMIN ME

I FINALLY FIGURED OUT THE ONLY REASON TO BE ALIVE IS TO ENJOY IT.

RITA MAE BROWN

IF OPPORTUNITY DOESN'T KNOCK, BUILD A DOOR.

MILTON BERLE

**FEAR IS
ONLY AS DEEP
AS THE MIND
ALLOWS.**

JAPANESE PROVERB

A POSITIVE
ATMOSPHERE
NURTURES A
POSITIVE ATTITUDE,
WHICH IS REQUIRED
TO TAKE POSITIVE
ACTION.

RICHARD DeVOS

OWN WHO
YOU ARE

*Be brave
enough
to be your
true self.*

QUEEN LATIFAH

I AM THE MASTER OF MY FATE: I AM THE CAPTAIN OF MY SOUL.

WILLIAM ERNEST HENLEY

I SAY IF I'M
BEAUTIFUL.
I SAY IF I'M
STRONG.
YOU WILL
NOT
DETERMINE
MY STORY.
I WILL.

AMY SCHUMER

YOU DON'T GET HARMONY WHEN EVERYBODY SINGS THE SAME NOTE.

ANONYMOUS

WHO YOU ARE
AUTHENTICALLY
IS ALL RIGHT.
WHO YOU ARE
IS BEAUTIFUL
AND AMAZING.

LAVERNE COX

IF WE ALL DID THE
THINGS WE ARE
CAPABLE OF, WE
WOULD LITERALLY
ASTOUND
OURSELVES.

THOMAS EDISON

Life is tough, but so are you

BE SO GOOD
THEY CAN'T
IGNORE YOU.

STEVE MARTIN

I think it's very important to do things the way you want to do them and be true to yourself, your own goals, and your own ideals.

ELISABETH MOSS

FIND OUT WHO YOU ARE AND DO IT ON PURPOSE.

DOLLY PARTON

CHANGE WILL NOT COME IF WE WAIT FOR SOME OTHER PERSON OR SOME OTHER TIME. WE ARE THE ONES WE'VE BEEN WAITING FOR.

BARACK OBAMA

DO YOUR THING AND DON'T CARE IF THEY LIKE IT.

TINA FEY

DO WHAT YOU
CAN, WITH
WHAT YOU'VE
GOT, WHERE
YOU ARE.

SQUIRE BILL WIDENER

THE THING EVERYONE SHOULD REALIZE IS THAT THE KEY TO HAPPINESS IS BEING HAPPY BY YOURSELF AND FOR YOURSELF.

ELLEN DeGENERES

DON'T BE
AFRAID TO
PUSH YOUR
BOUNDARIES

TELL ME, WHAT IS
IT YOU PLAN TO
DO WITH YOUR
ONE WILD AND
PRECIOUS LIFE?

MARY OLIVER

*Don't you ever let
a soul in the world
tell you that you
can't be exactly
who you are.*

LADY GAGA

YOUR LIFE

is a story –

MAKE

every chapter

COUNT

WHETHER YOU
COME FROM
A COUNCIL
ESTATE OR
A COUNTRY
ESTATE, YOUR
SUCCESS WILL
BE DETERMINED
BY YOUR OWN
CONFIDENCE.

MICHELLE OBAMA

IF YOU CAN DO WHAT YOU DO BEST AND BE HAPPY, YOU ARE FURTHER ALONG IN LIFE THAN MOST PEOPLE.

LEONARDO DiCAPRIO

CREATE THE KIND OF SELF THAT YOU WILL BE HAPPY TO LIVE WITH ALL YOUR LIFE.

GOLDA MEIR

FIND SOMETHING
YOU'RE
PASSIONATE
ABOUT AND KEEP
TREMENDOUSLY
INTERESTED IN IT.

JULIA CHILD

Only you have the power to change your future

WE ALWAYS
MAY BE WHAT
WE MIGHT
HAVE BEEN.

ADELAIDE ANNE PROCTER

WE HAVE TO DARE
TO BE OURSELVES,
HOWEVER
FRIGHTENING OR
STRANGE THAT SELF
MAY PROVE TO BE.

MAY SARTON

YOU'RE ONLY
= *confined by* =
THE WALLS
= *you build* =
YOURSELF

You don't need anybody to tell you who you are or what you are. You are what you are!

JOHN LENNON

WHAT YOU DO TODAY CAN IMPROVE ALL YOUR TOMORROWS.

RALPH MARSTON

IT'S NOT YOUR JOB TO LIKE ME – IT'S MINE.

BYRON KATIE

I'M GONNA LOOK BACK ON MY LIFE AND SAY THAT I ENJOYED IT – AND I LIVED IT FOR ME.

RIHANNA

DO ONE THING EVERY DAY THAT SCARES YOU, UNTIL IT DOESN'T

SELF-TRUST IS THE FIRST SECRET OF SUCCESS.

RALPH WALDO EMERSON

NOTHING CAN
DIM THE LIGHT
WHICH SHINES
FROM WITHIN.

MAYA ANGELOU

*I can
and
I will*

BE YOURSELF.
DO WHATEVER
YOU WANT TO
DO AND DON'T
LET BOUNDARIES
HOLD YOU BACK.

SOPHIE TURNER

You will never do anything in this world without courage. It is the greatest quality of the mind next to honour.

ARISTOTLE

SELF-CONFIDENCE IS THE FIRST REQUISITE TO GREAT UNDERTAKINGS.

SAMUEL JOHNSON

MY MOTTO IS:
I'M ALIVE,
SO THAT MEANS
I CAN DO
ANYTHING.

VENUS WILLIAMS

Above all, trust yourself

ORDINARY ME
CAN ACHIEVE
SOMETHING
EXTRAORDINARY
BY GIVING
THAT LITTLE
BIT EXTRA.

BEAR GRYLLS

YOU'RE PERFECT WHEN YOU'RE COMFORTABLE BEING YOURSELF.

ANSEL ELGORT

LIFE DOESN'T HAPPEN TO YOU; YOU HAPPEN TO LIFE

THE MORE YOU
PRAISE AND
CELEBRATE
YOUR LIFE, THE
MORE THERE
IS IN LIFE TO
CELEBRATE.

OPRAH WINFREY

THERE IS NO ONE
ALIVE THAT IS
YOU-ER THAN YOU.

Dr SEUSS

A good head and a good heart are always a formidable combination.

NELSON MANDELA

*IT'S ALL RIGHT
TO HAVE
BUTTERFLIES
IN YOUR
STOMACH. JUST
GET THEM
TO FLY IN
FORMATION.*

ROB GILBERT

YOU

ARE

ALL KINDS

OF

MARVELLOUS

I DON'T WANT OTHER PEOPLE TO DECIDE WHO I AM. I WANT TO DECIDE THAT FOR MYSELF.

EMMA WATSON

I DON'T THINK LIMITS.

USAIN BOLT

STRIVE
for
THE LIFE
you want
TO LIVE

ALL WE HAVE TO DECIDE IS WHAT TO DO WITH THE TIME THAT IS GIVEN TO US.

J. R. R. TOLKIEN

**BEWARE;
FOR I AM
FEARLESS
AND
THEREFORE
POWERFUL.**

MARY SHELLEY

LIVE BOLDLY.
PUSH YOURSELF.
DON'T SETTLE.

JOJO MOYES

YOU CAN,
YOU SHOULD,
AND IF YOU'RE
BRAVE ENOUGH
TO START,
YOU WILL.

STEPHEN KING

The sky
is not
the limit;
there are
endless
galaxies

One can never consent to creep when one feels an impulse to soar.

HELEN KELLER

THIS ABOVE ALL: TO THINE OWN SELF BE TRUE.

WILLIAM SHAKESPEARE

NOTE
─── *to* ───
SELF:
─── *I am* ───
ENOUGH

THE FORMULA OF HAPPINESS AND SUCCESS IS JUST BEING ACTUALLY YOURSELF, IN THE MOST VIVID POSSIBLE WAY YOU CAN.

MERYL STREEP

BE YOURSELF. THE WORLD WORSHIPS THE ORIGINAL.

INGRID BERGMAN

YOU MUST
NEVER BE
FEARFUL
ABOUT WHAT
YOU ARE
DOING WHEN
IT IS RIGHT.

ROSA PARKS

THERE'S POWER IN LOOKING SILLY AND NOT CARING THAT YOU DO.

AMY POEHLER

SHOW

YOUR

DOUBTS

WHAT YOU'RE

MADE OF!

FOLLOW YOUR PASSIONS, FOLLOW YOUR HEART, AND THE THINGS YOU NEED WILL COME.

ELIZABETH TAYLOR

When you become
the image of your
own imagination,
it's the most
powerful thing
you could ever do.

RuPAUL

You don't
have to
be perfect
to be
amazing

ONE WHO
WALKS IN
ANOTHER'S
TRACKS
LEAVES NO
FOOTPRINTS.

PROVERB

POSITIVITY,
CONFIDENCE AND
PERSISTENCE ARE
KEY IN LIFE, SO
NEVER GIVE UP
ON YOURSELF.

KHALID

When there's rain, make your own sunshine

DO WHAT YOU WERE BORN TO DO. YOU HAVE TO TRUST YOURSELF.

BEYONCÉ

LISTEN TO YOUR INNER VOICE

ONE FINDS LIMITS BY PUSHING THEM.

HERBERT A. SIMON

**STOP TRYING
TO DEFINE
WHO YOU ARE
AND JUST BE.**

CARA DELEVINGNE

IF YOU DON'T
LIVE YOUR LIFE,
THEN WHO WILL?

RIHANNA

You are never too old to set another goal or to dream a new dream.

LES BROWN

MAKE A
wish...
THEN MAKE
it come
TRUE!

I... DO NOT.
BELONG.
TO ANYONE.
BUT MYSELF.
AND NEITHER
DO YOU.

ARIANA GRANDE

DOUBT WHOM YOU WILL, BUT NEVER YOURSELF.

CHRISTIAN NESTELL BOVEE

BE

YOU,

FOR

YOU

IF YOU HAVE AN IDEA, YOU HAVE TO BELIEVE IN YOURSELF OR NO ONE ELSE WILL.

SARAH MICHELLE GELLAR

DO A LITTLE MORE EACH DAY THAN YOU THINK YOU POSSIBLY CAN.

LOWELL THOMAS

WHAT I'M LOOKING FOR IS NOT OUT THERE, IT IS IN ME.

HELEN KELLER

DON'T LET THE
NOISE OF OTHERS'
OPINIONS DROWN
OUT YOUR OWN
INNER VOICE.

STEVE JOBS

BE

a

VOICE,

not an

ECHO

Man cannot discover new oceans unless he has the courage to lose sight of the shore.

ANDRÉ GIDE

IF YOU'RE PRESENTING YOURSELF WITH CONFIDENCE, YOU CAN PULL OFF PRETTY MUCH ANYTHING.

KATY PERRY

CHANGE TAKES COURAGE.

ALEXANDRIA OCASIO-CORTEZ

Good things come to those who... go out and get them!

BE BRAVE,
BE BOLD,
BE FREE.

ANGELINA JOLIE

LOVE YOURSELF
FIRST AND
EVERYTHING ELSE
FALLS INTO LINE.

LUCILLE BALL